YOU CHOOSE
BOOKS

EARLY AMERICAN BATTLES

AT THE BATTLE OF BULL RUN

AN INTERACTIVE BATTLEFIELD ADVENTURE

by Eric Braun

Consultant:
Richard Bell, PhD
Associate Professor of History
University of Maryland, College Park

CAPSTONE PRESS
a capstone imprint

You Choose Books are published by Capstone Press,
1710 Roe Crest Drive, North Mankato, Minnesota 56003
www.mycapstone.com

Library of Congress Cataloging-in-Publication Data
Library of Congress Cataloging-in-Publication data is available on the Library of
Congress website.

978-1-5435-0291-6 (library binding)
978-1-5435-0295-4 (paperback)
978-1-5435-0299-2 (eBook PDF)

Editorial Credits
Adrian Vigliano, editor; Bobbie Nuytten, designer;
Kelli Lageson, media researcher; Kathy McColley, production specialist

Photo Credits
Alamy: Paul Fearn, 83; Bridgeman Images: Private Collection/Look and Learn,
75, Private Collection/Peter Newark Military Pictures, 93, Private Collection/
Troiani, Don (b. 1949), Cover, 6, 34, 42, 60, 66; Library of Congress Prints
and Photographs Division: 14, 30, 49, 70, 100; National Archives and Records
Administration/WAR AND CONFLICT: 10, 25; Shutterstock: Alexey Pushkin,
Design Element, Atlantis Images, Design Element, Everett Historical, 38, 55,
Lukasz Szwaj, Design Element; Wikimedia: United States National Archives and
Records Administration, 103; XNR Productions: 53

Printed in the United States of America.
010830S18

Table of Contents

ABOUT YOUR ADVENTURE

You are living through a pivotal time in the history of the United States. The country has split into two parts as Southern states have seceded, or left, the country. The result is a new war, the Civil War, fought between the North and the South. Both sides are preparing for the war's first major battle. Can you survive this bloody time?

In this book you'll explore how the choices people made meant the difference between life and death. The events you'll experience happened to real people.

Chapter One sets the scene. Then you choose which path to read. Follow the directions at the bottom of each page. The choices you make will change your outcome. After you finish your path, go back and read the others for new perspectives and more adventures.

YOU CHOOSE the path
you take through history.

THE WAR IS PICKING UP

You are heading to battle. You walk along a pitted dirt road with your company. Ahead of you carriages weighed down with equipment creak and kick up dust. Dust is everywhere — it coats your face, it gets in your mouth. Officers bark directions while their horses dot the road with their poop. You and your fellow soldiers walk in silence, thinking about the fight ahead.

What will happen to you? Will you be brave or will you crumble under pressure? Will you live or die? And how will this war end?

Turn the page.

Most believe it will end soon, though it has barely begun. The North has more soldiers and more money. Northerners find it hard to imagine that the South will last long against these odds. At the same time, Southerners believe the North will eventually tire of a long-term invasion and will give up the fight.

But as you reach your position outside Manassas Junction, a growing chaos reaches your ears. The low thunder of hundreds of horse hooves rumbles the ground. You hear the clanging of mallets driving steel tent pegs and the "thock" of axes sinking into tree trunks. The most ominous sound is that of the heavy wheels of artillery moving into place.

You want to believe, like so many others, that this will be a short war. But as the earth rumbles with the movement of armies, you begin to fear that the bloodshed has only just begun.

To be a slave forced to fight for the South, turn to page 11.

To be a poor Confederate soldier from the mountains of North Carolina, turn to page 43.

To be a Northern woman disguised as a Union soldier, turn to page 71.

The 26th Regiment United States Colored Infantry was one of three African-American infantry units from New York that fought in the Civil War.

CHAPTER 2

SEEKING FREEDOM IN BATTLE

The white men watch you carefully. You feel their eyes on you at all times, even though you are on the same side. They don't trust you.

Of course this makes sense. They should not trust you.

When the war broke out, Master Carhardt ordered you to join the Confederate Army. Carhardt was the white man who owned you and your family and the Virginia plantation where you were enslaved. Now you have been forced to fight to preserve the cruel system of slavery.

Turn the page.

At first you and several other slaves were assigned to build cannons. You were not given weapons out of fear that you might use them to escape. Then General P. G. T. Beauregard learned from a spy that the Union planned to cut off the railroad at Manassas Junction, Virginia. The Confederates knew they had to confront the Union — and they needed more fighters. So you were trained for battle. You and Augustus, another enslaved man from Carhardt's plantation, are trained to fire a cannon you built. The type of cannon you're assigned to is heavy and made for long-range firing.

Other troops have built a wooden barricade along Bull Run Creek, and you push your cannon behind it. Augustus begins lifting cannon balls off a wagon and setting them near the cannon's muzzle. After checking to make sure none of the white men will hear, he speaks quietly to you.

"You hear the rumor?" he asks.

You shake your head. You noticed Augustus whispering with other slaves during the march north. It seems he has found out something big.

"Carhardt and both his boys went off to fight," Augustus says. He explains that all the white men have left the plantation. They left only white women and children behind to watch the slaves. With little security to hold them back, many of the slaves escaped. "I heard Rebecca and Janie got out," he says. That's your wife and baby daughter. You hope he's right.

You are shocked and thrilled. But there is little time to think about your family because cannon fire explodes through the air. A huge cloud of mud and water flies into the air downstream from you.

Turn the page.

Two soldiers of an African-American unit take aim and fire in Dutch Gap, Virginia.

A white soldier, Captain Pickens, orders you to fire on a Union artillery nest. You can see the target across the field in the trees. You realize those Union soldiers are fighting to free *you*.

To fire on them as ordered, turn to page 15.

To intentionally miss, turn to page 17.

Explosions rattle the earth and you are scared to the bone. You don't feel right about shooting at men who are fighting to end slavery but you have little choice. If you're caught sabotaging the attack, you'll be hanged. So you aim the gun. Augustus loads it with a solid ball and you fire.

The gun's roar echoes in your ears. For a moment you can't see or hear anything as you hunch with your eyes closed. When you look again, the enemy artillery nest is in flames. A feeling of sickness fills your stomach. You're sure you have killed someone.

There is little time to contemplate what is happening because ordnance fire rips through the air again. Just a few feet away, a section of the barricade explodes. You watch in horror as two slaves lie in the dirt screaming in pain. At least one of them seems to be fatally injured.

Turn the page.

You also see the body of the white captain who ordered you to shoot. An explosion flung him away from the others, closer to you. He is dead. You look around. No other officers are present for the moment.

To try to escape, turn to page 18.

To help the injured slaves, turn to page 20.

You can't bring yourself to kill Union soldiers. You wish you could fight alongside them. So after Augustus loads the cannon, you aim it in the enemy's direction. But you lower the muzzle so the shot will land low.

The cannonball explodes harmlessly in the dirt just on the other side of the stream. You and Augustus look at each other. You give him a look that tells him you did it on purpose.

"You there!" shouts the white officer, Captain Pickens. He looks furious. "I told you to fire on that artillery nest. I know you missed on purpose. I'll have you strung up!"

You look around. You are surrounded by black soldiers and they are looking at you.

To apologize and tell Captain Pickens it was a mistake, turn to page 21.

To tell him you refuse to fire on Union soldiers, turn to page 23.

You grab Augustus by the arm and point at the dead officer, Captain Pickens. "Now's our chance," you say.

There is a house along the creek not far downstream. Near it, a few families are sitting in the grass picnicking and watching the fighting. You run along the barricade toward them as gunfire and artillery fire rock the air. Hundreds of Union troops are advancing toward the Confederate position you just left. It looks like the Union will win this battle.

As you approach the house, an older woman sitting in a chair on the porch waves her hands at you. Is she welcoming you or telling you to go away? You can't tell. You don't know if she's sympathetic to the North or the South, but you decide to take a chance.

"Will you hide us?" you ask.

The woman stands up. "It's not safe for you here," she whispers. "Rebels have —"

Before she can finish, three white Confederate soldiers come out of the house.

"Well, well," says one, reaching for his pistol.

The woman steps in front of him. "No!"

Not far behind the house, the forest is thick. If you can make it there, you can escape in the woods. The Union camp can't be far. They will protect you if you can make it there.

19

To wait and see if the woman will convince the rebels to let you go, turn to page 24.

To run for it, turn to page 26.

The injured men lie moaning in the dirt. You can't just leave them. You rush to the dying man and help him sit up. You offer him water but he just gasps and coughs. Within a minute he is dead.

The other man is bleeding from his stomach and leg but looks like he will live. You bring him the water and Augustus presses a cloth to the wound in his belly. As the three of you hunch behind the barricade, you hear running footsteps. Peering over the top, you see Union soldiers running toward you. Some are firing their rifles. Others have bayonets ready. Wounded and dying Confederate soldiers are scattered all around. The remaining men flee.

You, Augustus, and the injured man huddle behind the barricade. The advancing soldiers look like they'll kill anyone in their path.

To retreat with the other Confederates, turn to page 28.

To wait for the Union soldiers, turn to page 31.

"I'm sorry, sir," you say. "The gun misfired. We'll get it right on the next shot."

You tell Augustus to load another cannonball, hoping that Captain Pickens will leave you to your work. Instead, you feel the tip of his sword at your throat.

"Sorry won't do," Pickens says. You feel a sharp pain as his sword cuts into your skin.

"Please, sir," Augustus says, "we will do better if you give us a chance."

Just then you hear another explosion and troops yelling. The rebel line seems to be breaking down. The barricade is burning, men are lying injured all over, and many other soldiers are retreating. Captain Pickens says, "This is your fault!"

Turn the page.

So many Confederates have retreated that the battlefield seems quiet for the moment. Union soldiers still advance, but they are walking instead of running. One Northerner stops by a dead Confederate and looks through his pockets. He takes something and slips it into his own pocket. For a moment, it seems that the war really will end quickly.

"I can't believe it," Pickens says, lowering his sword.

To make a run for it, turn to page 33.

To wait for orders from Captain Pickens, turn to page 35.

The other black soldiers seem to be looking to you for leadership. You decide to make a stand, even if it means risking your life.

"Captain Pickens," you say, "I can't rightly destroy those men. I'd sooner destroy myself."

Pickens spits on the ground, glares at you, and draws his sword. "You very well have done that."

He thrusts the blade into your belly. You look into his cruel eyes as pain spreads from your center. Your vision flickers. But as the world grows darker, you see a slave hit Pickens from behind with a rifle butt. Another joins in, knocking the officer to the ground. The last thing you see before you die is a dozen former slaves running to freedom.

23

THE END

To follow another path, turn to page 9.
To read the conclusion, turn to page 101.

"Don't hurt them!" the woman says, but the soldier pushes her aside. She stumbles back and watches as he aims his pistol at you.

The other two soldiers tie your hands with rope. They begin to lead you back toward the fighting line but a massive battle is going on. You get caught in a crossfire and drop to the ground.

As bullets whiz overhead, the soldier with the pistol lifts his head to look around. He aims his gun, fires, and grabs your arm. "Get up!" he says.

Fires burn in several areas on the battlefield and many men lie dead on the ground. Flies buzz around their bodies. Smoke drifts in the air. The fighting seems to be dying down. The Union has retreated and General Thomas Jackson's men have pursued them across the stone bridge. It looks bad — a Confederate victory and you and Augustus have lost your chance to escape.

General Thomas Jackson became widely known as "Stonewall" Jackson after reports of his actions at the Battle of Bull Run.

Worse yet, you don't know what fate is waiting for you. Will you be hanged? Forced back into slavery? Left to rot in prison? You only hope that Rebecca and Janie are safe.

THE END

To follow another path, turn to page 9.
To read the conclusion, turn to page 101.

You don't give yourself time to rethink it —
you just run for the end of the porch. The white
men shout at you as you turn the corner and
sprint to the trees. Augustus is right behind you.

A gunshot rings through the air and you see a
tree trunk burst ahead as the bullet hits it. Heavy
footsteps are behind you, but within seconds
you're in the forest. It's too thick for a bullet to
get far. They'll have to catch you by hand.

You veer into a thicket of bushes and tall
trees. Thorns and branches slash at your face but
your uniform protects the rest of your skin. You
can hear Augustus panting — he's right beside
you. But suddenly he trips into a soft marsh and
lands on his wrist. His hand dangles at a bad
angle when he stands again. He moans in pain
and he wobbles like he might pass out. Behind
you, your pursuers crash through the bushes.

"Come on," you say, pulling Augustus' good arm over your shoulders. You help him up a small hill where you find a huge, hollowed-out tree. You hide inside and wait in silence. You hear the soldiers hollering but they don't find you. After dark you make your way to the Union camp and surrender.

A Union captain and two other soldiers question you about your company. "Where did you march from?" the captain asks. "How many are there? What else do you know?"

You answer their questions and when you are finished, they thank you for your help. You are offered a job with the Union Army as a cook.

To take the job, turn to page 37.

To go to Washington, D.C., to look for your family, turn to page 39.

The shooting and screaming fill you with fear. Can you really just sit here and hope the Union soldiers don't kill or imprison you? You haven't met many white men you could trust. So you and Augustus lift the injured man together. You work your way slowly away from the front line toward the road you marched in on. You don't know where you're going — you just follow everyone else.

You've been walking for more than an hour when you realize that many of the rebels have stopped their retreat. You see that some have gone back to fight. You keep walking. Soon the road is empty except for you, Augustus, and the wounded man, whose name is Harper. The three of you hide in the woods until late at night. You clean and bandage Harper's wounds with torn-up shirts and water from a creek.

After nightfall you get up and begin walking east, knowing that eventually you will reach the Potomac River. When you do, you follow it north until you reach Washington, D.C. You walk only at night, hiding during daylight. You eat berries and tree bark. You are covered in mosquito bites, cuts from brambles and thorny bushes, and bruises from falling in the dark.

But after several days, you reach the city. At a newsstand you read about the battle, which is over now. The Confederates drove the Union armies out of Manassas Junction. This reporter calls the Union retreat "The Great Skedaddle."

You realize the war will be a long and bloody conflict, not the short one that many were predicting. You are torn between two strong desires. Part of you wants to find your family while the other wants to join the Union Army.

Turn the page.

An African-American soldier stands guard over a cannon in 1864.

You want to fight to end the enslavement of black people. You are a good cannon operator and you know you could be a real asset to the North. But for now you are exhausted. You can think only of sleep and food. For one night at least, you hope not to run or fight.

THE END

To follow another path, turn to page 9.
To read the conclusion, turn to page 101.

You huddle for protection behind the barricade and wait. You hope the Union soldiers will understand that you're only fighting for the Confederates because you've been forced to. Mostly likely they will help you get to freedom — or fight for the Union side.

The white Confederates flee toward the road, leaving you with Augustus and the wounded man. You consider running now because nobody knows where you are. You could disappear into the woods and no one would know. But eventually the Confederates would figure out that you're missing. They would try to hunt you down.

The Union men sweep in yelling and firing their rifles. You watch in shock as one Northerner attacks a fleeing rebel with his bayonet. The rebel falls, bleeding, in the grass.

Turn the page.

They haven't seen you yet. Augustus rises to his feet and calls out: "Over here!" A Union soldier turns and fires. Augustus collapses beside you, shot in the chest.

"Stop!" you yell. "We are friendly!"

But another shot rings out and suddenly you feel a burning pain rip your own chest. Blood spreads over the front of your Confederate uniform and your vision blurs. As you lose consciousness for the last time, you wish you had removed the uniform when you had the chance.

THE END

To follow another path, turn to page 9.
To read the conclusion, turn to page 101.

Pickens seems to be shocked that Beauregard's army is being pushed back. The Confederates seem to be losing — badly. While he looks across the field at the advancing enemy, you take a cautious step away. He doesn't turn toward you, so you run. You're not sure where you're going. You just concentrate on moving as quickly as you can.

Reaching an opening in the barricade, you and Augustus cut through it. Unfortunately it leads you right into the middle of the battlefield. You realize too late that you will almost surely be killed out here in the crossfire. For just a second, you pause. You consider going back to safety and taking your chances with Pickens. But going back means going back to fighting for a cause you hate and possibly dying for it. And if you survive the war, all that awaits you is a return to slavery.

Turn the page.

A Confederate officer signals to his soldiers as he leads them into battle.

Bullets whiz past your head. Smoke floats in the air. Augustus has already run deep into the chaos of the battlefield. You can't see him. You take a deep breath and run into the smoke.

THE END

To follow another path, turn to page 9.
To read the conclusion, turn to page 101.

Just when it seems the Union will win easily, you hear many men yelling out a wild battle cry. From the west Confederate General Jackson and his men begin furiously returning fire on the Union. The Northern soldiers look stunned and a few drop to the ground for protection. Some fire back.

"Fire!" Pickens says, gesturing at the cannon. You and Augustus load and fire into the mass of Union blue in front of you. Bodies fall and suddenly the Union men are retreating. Pickens grins. "Fire again!"

The Union troops are in full retreat now. You watch as Jackson and his men pursue them across the creek and across the field. Within an hour the fighting has died down and the Confederates have claimed victory.

Turn the page.

Back at the camp, Pickens tells you and the other men in your company, "If the Yanks thought it was going to be easy, they underestimated us! Fight on, men!"

You are assigned the job of helping to process prisoners of war. You collect their weapons and personal items like pocket knives and letters from their families. You can't help thinking of your own family. Where are they now? You may never know. For now you are working against your own freedom.

THE END

To follow another path, turn to page 9.
To read the conclusion, turn to page 101.

They put you in a tent with black soldiers. After Augustus' arm is wrapped and set, he falls into a deep sleep on the cot next to you. But you don't sleep — you lie awake thinking.

When Augustus wakes in the morning, he tells you that he is going on to Washington, D.C. He wants to see if his own family has made it there. You tell him that you've accepted the captain's offer to work for the Union Army.

"If you see Rebecca and Janie, tell them to wait for me in D.C.," you say. "I'll find them when all this fighting is done."

You serve the rest of the war with the captain's unit, first as a cook and later as a soldier. The war is long and bloody. You see many terrible battles, many deaths and injuries, and a few important victories.

Turn the page.

A group of former slaves who escaped the South volunteered to fight for the Union in 1863.

Finally, in 1865 the North wins the war. You feel deep pride for your role in preserving the Union and ending slavery.

You reach Washington, D.C., after four years of war. You have never heard anything from Augustus or your family and you fear they never made it. But as you step off the train into a sunny afternoon, you feel hopeful. Maybe you will find them.

THE END

To follow another path, turn to page 9.
To read the conclusion, turn to page 101.

You thank the captain for his offer, but then explain why you must go. You know you can't stay here when your wife and child may need you.

The next night you and Augustus begin walking toward Washington, D.C. After walking for two nights and hiding during the day, you arrive at the outskirts of the city. Augustus knows of a tavern where escaped slaves are sometimes sheltered and often leave messages. So you creep through the streets, hiding in dark alleys when you see people, until you reach the tavern. Augustus knocks and you wait nervously, hoping to find a friendly face on the other side.

A white man lets you inside. He leads you to a secret room in the basement, where you talk by candlelight.

Turn the page.

The man, Jonah, has met Rebecca and Janie. He knows where they are hiding. Your heart thrills at this news. But Jonah has heard no word of Augustus' family and your joy is tempered by a deep sadness for your friend.

The next night you find your family. Janie has grown so much you can hardly believe it. You and Rebecca decide to leave for Canada as soon as possible. As escaped slaves, Canada is the only truly safe place for you. Jonah supplies you with a little money, some dried meat, and a map to safe houses along the way.

Traveling by night, you reach Buffalo, New York, after many weeks. In a safe house there, you are introduced to a newspaper reporter who asks to interview you. He promises to change your name and the route of your escape so the story can't be used to find you.

So you tell him about the pain and horror of slavery and about your time as a soldier. You hope the story will show the country how evil slavery is. Maybe it will help rally more volunteers to the Union Army or encourage more white people to help fleeing slaves.

The next night you take a small boat and row by moonlight across the Niagara River. At last you reach the far shore. When you step out of the boat, you are in Canada. You and your family are finally free.

THE END

To follow another path, turn to page 9.
To read the conclusion, turn to page 101.

A typical Confederate infantry soldier in 1861.

CHAPTER 3

A RICH MAN'S WAR BUT A POOR MAN'S FIGHT

The company stops marching for a rest and you pull out your bag of walnuts. Reaching into the sack, you sift your fingers through the nuts and relax slightly. Your two brothers take off their packs and rest next to you.

"You and those nuts," says your younger brother, Andrew, while your older brother, Newell, laughs. "Why don't you just eat them?"

Turn the page.

Andrew and the others think it's strange that you carry this small satchel of walnuts in your pack everywhere you go. They add weight to your burden and they are crushed from all the marching. You don't eat them. You simply feel them every now and then. They come from your walnut tree back home in the Ozark Mountains. They remind you of better days. You used to climb that tree as a boy. On special occasions your mother would make walnut bars with sugar and the apples that also grew on your land. You'd think your brothers would understand.

Your family also raised potatoes, squash, beans, watermelons, and wheat, along with four hogs. You hunted deer and wild birds for extra meat. Life in the mountains was hard but pleasant. You never imagined going anywhere else but since joining the Confederate Army, you have seen a lot.

All the men in your company are poor, just like you and both of your brothers. You're proud men from the piney mountains who are familiar with hard work. None of you owns any slaves. If you are successful, maybe one day you will.

In the late afternoon, you are awakened by the sound of men talking excitedly. You look across the farm field and the creek to where they are pointing. There you see what must be several thousand Union troops marching, their bayonets glinting in the sun. Your officers announce that your unit is to retreat to a river crossing called Mitchell's Ford.

To retreat with your unit to Mitchell's Ford, turn to page 46.

To lead a small group of men doing reconnaissance at another crossing, turn to page 48.

You are greatly outnumbered here, so your company hastily lines up and begins to march. Passing through a trench in full view of the enemy, you all crouch low so they cannot see how few of you there are. Flags are dipped low too. As you emerge on the far side of the trench, you're ordered to march at "double-quick" time — nearly a run.

Union troops are in pursuit but an artillery unit fires shells to slow them down. Soon you are safely on the outskirts of a town called Centreville, where you are given time to rest. There is no water and occasionally you are ordered to stand at the ready. Everyone is tired, thirsty, and worried about the coming battle. But the Union troops never arrive, and once again you are ordered to march. By morning, you reach Mitchell's Ford.

All the maneuvering confuses you and your brothers and you're disappointed to be retreating. But the officers seem in good spirits. They think the retreat has lured the Union into over-confidence. Taking up positions near a stone bridge across the Bull Run River, you ready yourselves for battle.

Then you see it: Yankees advancing on the bridge. Your captain orders you to hold your fire until they draw near so as not to waste ammunition. But the Yankees see you and begin shooting. Newell is hit in the hand and cries out. You begin to panic.

To fire on the man who shot Newell, turn to page 50.

To wait, turn to page 52.

You march to Union Mills Ford. After determining that the crossing is safe for now, you rest for a few hours. Late that afternoon, you are ordered to take 20 men across the river to assess the enemy's position.

You hike into the river canyon in the shadow of a train bridge and wade across. On the enemy side, you sneak under the cover of bushes and boulders up to the edge of the road. You point your telescope through the bush and peer down the road.

You gasp. Dozens of Union wagons are moving along the road. Infantry soldiers line the road. Troops wheel artillery guns toward you.

"What is it?" one of the men asks.

"They're well-positioned here," you say, handing him the scope. "They have a large advantage."

Union officers meet to discuss war strategies.

"They'll obliterate our army unless we do something," the soldier says.

"Our instructions are to report back what we found," you say. But you agree now might be the best time to do something.

To return immediately and report what you've seen, turn to page 54.

To find a way to sabotage the Union Army, turn to page 56.

Newell whimpers in pain, but he wraps his bleeding hand and loads his weapon. You are filled with fury. You raise your loaded rifle to your shoulder and peer around the tree. You put an enemy soldier in your sight and squeeze the trigger, but you miss. Suddenly more Yankee bullets rain down on your position.

"Tanner, you mountain-bred idiot!" the captain hisses, "I told you to hold fire!"

You crouch behind your tree. All the white officers, most of whom are wealthy landowners, look down on poor folks from the mountains. You are even angrier than before, but you await orders.

The Yankees advance and at last the captain orders the attack. You wheel around your tree and fire your rifle. Several enemy soldiers drop with the volley of rifle fire. But the Northerners are too numerous and soon the captain has you retreating once again. You run close to your brothers for nearly an hour, shots whizzing through the air.

Finally, downriver you see General Thomas Jackson on his horse. He and his army are standing and fighting while other Confederate armies continue to retreat. A voice from among the officers says, "Yonder stands Jackson like a stone wall!"

To continue retreating with your company, turn to page 58.

To join Jackson and fight, turn to page 60.

You're not sure the captain is making the right choice but you obey your orders. The Union fires on you but you remain protected in the trees. Hundreds of Yankees pour over the bridge and soon they are nearly upon you. The captain orders a counterattack and you fire.

But there are too many Yankees and many have reached the woods where you're taking shelter. Several of them use bayonets to attack Confederates, stabbing and slashing. The captain orders a retreat and you begin to run.

Late that night, you regroup near a courthouse in a nearby town. Word spreads among the men that the retreat was part of a larger plan. With the Union troops feeling confident, they extended their attack too far. Confederate reinforcements are arriving right now and already the generals have begun to squeeze the Yankees in a trap.

But something is wrong. You can't find Andrew. After asking around, you find out your brother was shot in the retreat. He may be dead or injured.

To look for him, turn to page 63.

To stay in safety and wait for word, turn to page 65.

The North and the South both won important victories in 1861.

You lead your group back across the river and report your findings. Several officers discuss what to do next and your captain assigns you to guard a trailhead downriver.

You set up your post at the trailhead and wait. Before long, you hear guns firing near the stone bridge. Men are yelling, but at your post there is no action for a long time. You take out your bag of walnuts and sift your fingers through them.

Suddenly you think you hear footsteps. You take your hand out of the bag, stand, and listen. You hear it again — men are running on the trail. You point your rifle at the trailhead and a moment later five black soldiers come out of the woods.

A group of slaves arrive at a Union camp after escaping the South.

"Hold it!" you say. The men freeze. They look terrified. None of them says a word. You realize they must be slaves assigned to fight for the Confederates. It seems they have escaped in the chaos of battle.

To detain them with your rifle, turn to page 67.

To let them go, turn to page 69.

You decide to try to damage the Union position, hoping the captain will appreciate your initiative. So you wait a few hours until it is dark, and then you and your men sneak along the road to where the Yankees are camped. You split into four small groups and sneak up to the enemy supply wagons.

As you approach your targeted wagon, you see two infantrymen standing guard. You and Andrew sneak up behind them and hit them with your rifle butts. The guards collapse and you quickly sneak into the wagons and spill the kerosene lanterns inside. The wood catches fire and you move the stored gunpowder nearby so it will explode. At first it looks as if your mission is a success. Your wagon goes up in flames and you see another wagon go up seconds later.

As you are running back toward the bridge, Andrew is shot in the leg and collapses. You turn to help him and see that you are surrounded by Union soldiers. You are brought to a prison tent where you are guarded carefully.

In another tent across the road, you see officers laughing together — Union officers and a captured Confederate officer. The Confederate officer is eating with the Northerners and he is not shackled as you are. You realize all the officers on both sides are wealthy. And you've seen how they send poor soldiers like you to do the fighting. They talk about sacrificing for the greater good — the cause of protecting the South. And you foolishly believed them. Now you will spend the rest of the war in prison.

THE END

To follow another path, turn to page 9.
To read the conclusion, turn to page 101.

Your company makes a disorganized retreat all the way to the town of Fairfax, where you regroup with other units. Later you learn that after your company fled, General Jackson and his men helped drive back the Yankees from Manassas. Other units joined Jackson, forcing the Union troops all the way to Washington, D.C. It is a major victory for the Confederates. You feel ashamed you were not a part of it.

With the victory, the South is energized and motivated for a long, hard war. All hope of a quick ending has disappeared. You learn that your unit will be part of a campaign in the West.

You have one night to spend as you wish, so you go to a tavern carrying your bag of walnuts as usual. You think of home. You hope your mother is okay by herself.

The tavern keeper stops to watch you. "What's in the bag?" she asks.

"Walnuts," you say. Then you tell her about your farm back home. You tell her about your mother and what a good cook she is.

"Did you fight in the battle here?" she asks.

"I did," you reply.

She smiles. "You're very brave."

"I just do what they tell me," you say, shaking your head.

"I hope you see your farm again," she says.

"Thank you," you say. Already it is hard to remember what your mother looks like. Home seems very far away.

THE END

To follow another path, turn to page 9.
To read the conclusion, turn to page 101.

a Confederate soldier from the 4th Virginia Regiment

"Sir, let us join Jackson," you say. "We can win this battle."

The captain yells in anger: "We retreat!"

"I am joining him!" you yell back, starting off toward Jackson's unit.

Your captain hollers after you, "You will hang for this disobedience, Tanner!"

As you run across a field, bullets zip through the air. Something explodes behind you and you run even faster. Men lie dead or dying all around and you can smell the blood. You fall in with a group of Jackson's men who are firing from behind a mound of earth. You join them in shooting and soon the Union soldiers who had been advancing are turning back.

General Jackson leads you and the others in pursuit. You shoot a fleeing Yankee, and he falls. The Union continues to retreat, and Jackson calls off the pursuit. You have far fewer men than they do and sooner or later they will realize they can turn you back.

Turn the page.

Later, after returning to the camp, General Jackson himself shakes your hand and thanks you for your bravery. You have conflicting feelings. You are proud of yourself and thrilled that Jackson has recognized it. At the same time, you fear the horror of this war will haunt you for the rest of your life.

THE END

To follow another path, turn to page 9.
To read the conclusion, turn to page 101.

You and Newell run along the road in the dark, too worried to be careful about being seen. As you run, you pass dead soldiers lying in the road and in the bushes. You check each one to make sure it isn't Andrew. One man, another Confederate soldier, is not quite dead. He breathes heavily and when you approach he asks for water.

"I have no water," you say. "But we will return to bring you to safety."

At a bend in the road, you see a booted foot sticking out of the tall grass. You rush over and see that it is Andrew. He is bleeding from a gunshot wound in the arm but he's not badly hurt.

"What are you doing?" you ask. "You could have been killed."

Turn the page.

"I was out," Andrew says. "When I woke up, I just couldn't stand to go back. All I could think about was how pointless this fighting is. We had a good life back at home! Why do we want to fight in this war? Just so rich men can get what they want? Brother, this isn't our war, it's theirs!"

You help your brother to his feet and the three of you walk slowly back along the road. When you reach the injured soldier, he is dead.

"Curse this war," Newell says.

"Andrew," you say. "You are right. This war is not for us." A few minutes later, the decision is made. The three of you walk into the thick woods and begin to make your way home.

THE END

To follow another path, turn to page 9.
To read the conclusion, turn to page 101.

It's safer to stay here and wait. There are still skirmishes all over the area and you could easily be killed. You think of your mother. It would be hard enough for her to lose one of her sons. You hate to think how losing two — or all three — would crush her.

You can't sleep, so you sit on a cot and sift your fingers through your bag of walnuts. Newell lies near you on another cot. Later, you hear news that the tide of the battle turned. The Union is in full retreat. You are glad but it's hard to feel very excited.

The next morning, the captain comes into the tent.

"Boys," he says. "They found your brother. He was shot. He was bleeding badly on the side of the road. I'm sorry to say, he didn't make it."

Turn the page.

Confederate soldiers led by General Jackson march north toward Washington, D.C., in 1861.

Your throat tightens and tears fill your eyes.

"Where is he?" Newell asks.

"Buried in the woods where he fell. I'm sorry."

The captain is quiet for a moment while you and Newell absorb this news. Then he says, "Pack your gear. We march in 45 minutes." He leaves and you begin packing. There is no more time to grieve.

THE END

To follow another path, turn to page 9.
To read the conclusion, turn to page 101.

You raise your rifle. "Stop!"

The men stop and turn to look at you. They have scraps for clothes and they look thin and desperate. There are five of them and only one of you. You realize that if they wanted to attack you, you could probably only shoot one of them.

"What are you doing?" you ask.

"Sir," one of them says. "My wife and baby are in danger. I aim to find them."

"I aim to stop you," you say, not sure you can.

They clearly understand the same thing — you are outnumbered.

After a moment the man with the family speaks again: "We'll keep on going. You can only shoot one of us. The rest of us will get away."

Turn the page.

They back away from you toward a stand of brush and high grass. Then, one by one, they turn and slip into the grass and climb down the riverbank. They are gone. Something came over you, and you couldn't shoot any of them. Perhaps you didn't have the courage — or the cruelty — to do it. As the interaction plays out again in your mind, you begin to doubt the rightness of this war.

THE END

To follow another path, turn to page 9.
To read the conclusion, turn to page 101.

You realize that you are outnumbered. There are five of them and you don't know if they are armed. So you turn and walk the other way as if you never saw them. Behind you, you hear them pause and then slip down below the riverbank. When you look back, they're gone.

Back at the camp, your captain confronts you.

"Did you see those slaves? They were heading your way — you should have stopped them."

"I didn't see anything," you say nervously.

The captain steps so close you can smell his breath. "That's impossible," he snarls. He calls over two soldiers, who put you in a cell. You spend the rest of the war in prison.

THE END

To follow another path, turn to page 9.
To read the conclusion, turn to page 101.

Frances Clalin Clayton disguised herself and used the name Jack Williams in order to fight in the Union Army in 1861.

CHAPTER 4

UNDERCOVER

Your father wanted boys. He only got one —
your brother. He also got you — a strong, tough,
smart young woman. You have always worked
harder than your brother on your Minnesota
farm. You learned all the skills boys learn, such as
horseback riding, hunting, and fighting, but it was
never enough. Deep down, you know your father
never loved you the way he loves your brother.

When war broke out and President Lincoln
called for volunteers, you decided to answer. There
was only one problem. The army only takes men.
So you did the one thing you could think of that
made sense. You disguised yourself as a man.

Turn the page.

One night you cut your hair short. Then you saddled a horse and rode away. At the recruiting office, nobody questioned you when you told them your new, fake name: Quincy Helling.

You are assigned to an infantry unit and you begin training at a camp near your home in Minnesota. Some men in your company tease you because you can't grow a beard but you make a few friends. You receive basic medical training, which you pick up easily. You have lots of experience caring for your injured family members.

At the end of your training, you learn that you have been assigned to work as a nurse. This is disappointing to you because you wanted to fight for the Union. On the other hand, you have a real talent for nursing. It may be the best way you can help.

To ask your captain for a different assignment, turn to page 73.

To go for medical training, turn to page 76.

You approach the captain after morning drills. "I would like to fight, sir," you say.

The captain looks at you for a moment before replying. "Normally I would tell you to show respect and do what you're told," he says. "You don't get to pick your assignment. But in this case, there might actually be another option."

He tells you that Major Kelly had considered another role for you. Because you have proven yourself to be very smart, Kelly thought you would make a good spy. He tells you of a plan to enlist you in the Confederate Army. There, you would work to learn about troop movements, attack plans, and anything else that might be of value. Then you would relay that information back to the Union through secret messengers. It would be very dangerous. If you're caught, you would be tortured and probably killed.

Turn the page.

After meeting with Major Kelly, you agree to take the job. You work for a week with several trainers to learn your Southern identity. You are now disguised as Robert Brown, a shopkeeper's son from Tennessee. Your head spins with all the layers of pretending you have to do!

Finally you take a train into Ohio. There you meet an agent who gets you aboard a carriage that takes you to a small town in Kentucky. There you spend the night with a local family. The next day, two wagons stop at the house. They carry Southern men on their way to Virginia, where they plan to enlist in the Confederate Army. One of the men calls down to you: "Hurry, now. We've got a war to win!"

You climb onto the wagon.

Loreta Janeta Velazquez disguised herself as a man in order to fight with the Confederate Army.

Within three days you are in full Confederate uniform, marching with your company toward Manassas Junction. You work hard, and soon you become a second lieutenant. You believe your peers and superiors trust you completely.

To stay close to the major in charge of your company, turn to page 78.

To linger near the other officers, turn to page 80.

You find it strange but you do not get any additional medical training. You take a train to Washington, D.C. There, your unit is deployed to Manassas Junction for the battle at Bull Run. You set up a hospital tent and when the fighting begins, you have only one patient — a soldier with a fever. So you watch the battle.

You're not the only one watching. Near the road many families have come to picnic and watch the fighting. It disgusts you that they think this is entertainment. People's lives are at stake. The spectators cheer as the Union forces push the Confederates back toward the Bull Run River. The Confederate retreat is so rapid that many Union soldiers stop their pursuit. Some of them laugh and stop in the field to pick up mementos, such as guns dropped by the enemy soldiers.

You check on your patient but soon you notice the doctor staring at you. You are afraid he realizes you are a woman. Before he can say anything, you hear increased shooting and yelling outside. Back at the tent door, you see that the Confederates have reinforcements and are charging. The Union is retreating. Within moments, the hospital is busy with dozens of patients. More injured men are on their way. One man has had his knee completely shattered by a rifle bullet. His leg seems to need amputation. The doctor is busy with other patients, so you can't ask his opinion.

To clean and bandage the wound, turn to page 82.

To cut off the leg, turn to page 83.

At mealtime you sit close to Major Thompson and ask him questions about General Beauregard's battle plans. As you eat, Thompson tells you that General Johnston is bringing his army of 12,000 men to Manassas Gap to help crush the Union. The Union believes it will only be facing Beauregard's 20,000 men. This could turn the tide of the battle.

That night in camp, while other officers in your tent are asleep, you sneak out. You tell the guard that you are restless and need to take a walk. There is some activity in the camp — some men talk quietly, others sit in silence by their fires. One tent glows from inside. Officers must be having a meeting in there. You slip out of camp and onto the road, then into the woods to avoid more guards.

Soon you are hidden in the dark beneath the stone bridge at the river. Water rushes by below you. A man who should be your secret Union contact comes out of the shadows and says, "Robert Tad."

The password is "Robert Todd," the name of President Lincoln's oldest son. Tad is his youngest son. Did your contact make a mistake? Did you mishear him? Or is this an imposter who doesn't know the real password?

To tell the man what you learned from Major Thompson, turn to page 85.

If you don't trust him, turn to page 87.

Several lieutenants and Captain Pickens are sitting in front of a tent discussing the next day's battle. You join them.

"Please sit, Lieutenant Brown," Pickens says.

Keeping your voice low and quiet, you answer, "Thank you," and sit on a wooden crate. You copy the posture of the other men — knees wide, chin high.

"We were just talking about Captain Pickens' unit," one lieutenant says. Pickens is in charge of a unit of slaves assigned to artillery guns. But he's worried about what will happen in the heat of battle. Will they rise up and attack the white Confederates? Will they try to escape? Pickens believes they will try something.

Of course they will, you think. *It's better than being a slave.* But you say nothing.

Now Pickens is staring hard at you. "What is it?" you ask.

"There's something funny about you, Brown," he says.

"What do you mean?" you ask. "There's nothing funny about me."

"I've been watching you," he says, "and something isn't right."

The other men all look at you.

To try to change the subject, turn to page 90.

To stand up to him, turn to page 92.

The doctor seems to prefer amputation as his main treatment option — he has removed several limbs from other men already. Your patient sees this and begs you not to remove his leg. So you clean the wound and wrap it in a bandage to stop the bleeding. Then you move to another soldier who is bleeding from a shot to the stomach.

You remove the bullet and press bandages to his belly but the soldier does not stop bleeding. He begins to cry and wail.

"Leave him!" the doctor says. "He's as good as dead. I need your help with these men who have a chance to live."

"No!" cries the dying man. "Don't leave me. Help me!"

To help the doctor, turn to page 95.
To stay with the dying man, turn to page 98.

"Don't cut it off!" the soldier cries when he sees the saw. But you know it is the only way to save his life. You give him a dose of ether, which calms him down and eases his pain. Then you tie him to the table so he won't be able to move during the operation.

Anna Bell served as a nurse during the Civil War.

Turn the page.

You tie a tourniquet above the knee to stanch the bleeding, and then you begin. Blood seeps onto the table and floor, and the man wails in pain. Finally it is done. You give the man more ether to help with the pain.

Suddenly you feel very ill, and you run outside to throw up. When you stand again, you're ready to get back to work when you see another wave of injured soldiers coming your way in the backs of wagons. The company musicians have been given the job of pulling these wagons and collecting the wounded. It is obvious that you will cut off more limbs before the day is through and you will see many men die. You will hear their anguished screams all day, all night, and for the rest of your life. It will be a long, gruesome war.

THE END

To follow another path, turn to page 9.
To read the conclusion, turn to page 101.

84

You look carefully at the man. He is dressed in shop-made clothes — a good sign that he is from a city in the North. You decide his password was close enough. It might even be *you* who has it wrong. Either way, you want to do everything you can to deliver the information to the Union generals. You know it's very important.

"Big news," you tell the man. "Johnston is moving 12,000 men to the junction." After relaying all the details, the man thanks you.

"Y'all be safe now," he says. Was that a Southern accent? You don't know but it's too late now. You rush back to your tent and slip inside. In the coming days, Johnston's men reinforce Beauregard's men, just as planned. The Union seems totally unprepared for this and their troops are forced into retreat.

Turn the page.

What happened to your message? Does someone in the Confederacy know your secret? You decide you must be even more careful from now on. You do not attempt to make contact with anyone from the Union. You feel like you're under constant suspicion. Are they waiting to trap you? What will they do if they catch you? Soon the pressure is so great, you feel you must get out before something terrible happens to you.

Several nights after the battle at the junction, your company is camping in Virginia. Just like you did so many nights ago, you leave camp for a walk. Only this time you are not meeting anyone. You are running for your life.

THE END

To follow another path, turn to page 9.
To read the conclusion, turn to page 101.

It sounded like the man spoke with a slight Southern accent. "What are you doing here, stranger?" you ask.

"What news do you have?" he replies.

"No news, sir. What do you mean?"

He says nothing. He touches the butt of his holstered pistol and you feel a sense of terror creep up your spine. But he does not draw. Finally, he says, "Good night, then," and disappears into the shadows.

You wait for a few seconds to let your heart settle down and then you scramble up the bank. You sneak undetected back into camp and go to sleep in your bedroll.

Turn the page.

When the battle begins, the Union soldiers pour over the stone bridge and push the Confederates back up the hill. But Beauregard's troops hold them off long enough for Johnston to arrive with his army. Soon the Union troops are retreating. Dozens of Union soldiers fall injured and dead on the hill.

You feel guilty for not delivering the message that could have helped the North. Nearby you see a Union soldier crumple near the bottom of the hill. Wanting to help somehow, you rush down the hill and begin dragging the man to safety. But before you get far, you feel a searing pain rip into your ribs — you've been shot too. You collapse in the dirt, breathing heavily, and within a minute you have lost consciousness.

When you wake you're in a Confederate hospital. A doctor is ripping at your shirt so he can attend to the wound. You begin to panic. Not wanting to be discovered as a woman, you roll away.

You muster all of your strength and get off the table. "I'll be fine," you say. You walk to your tent. You realize you should have let the doctor treat you. You are bleeding badly and if you don't get help, you'll die. Someone says your name — your real name: "Martha."

It is your father. But how can that be true? How can he be here? You must be hallucinating. Your father's voice is the last sound you hear before dying.

THE END

To follow another path, turn to page 9.
To read the conclusion, turn to page 101.

You laugh as if the captain was making a joke. Then you try turning the conversation back to the subject of slaves in the company. "There are so many of them," you say. "If they decide to revolt, surely they can overwhelm us."

Captain Pickens chuckles quietly. He understands you are avoiding his comments. He seems to think a moment, then he dismisses the rest of the officers: "Leave us."

When the others have gone, Pickens says, "Madam, what is your real name?" Your fingers go cold from fear.

"Wh-what do you mean?"

"Don't be afraid," he says, looking around cautiously. "I admire what you've done. You wanted to fight for our cause, but the army didn't take women. You're very brave."

So he knows you're a woman — but not that you're a Union spy. He tells you your secret is safe with him and he agrees to help you protect it.

Over the ensuing months, you and Pickens become very close. As a captain he has access to a lot of information. He knows about attack plans, troop movements, and weapons factories. He shares much of this information with you. Little does he know that you pass along all these secrets to your contacts in the North. You can only hope that the war will end a little sooner because of your daring work.

THE END

To follow another path, turn to page 9.
To read the conclusion, turn to page 101.

You stand up and ball your fists. "What are you trying to say, sir?"

Without getting up or looking the least bit worried, he says, "Sit down, lieutenant."

"Well, there's nothing *funny* about me and I don't like you saying there is." You decide that a man would not back down without an apology, so you step closer to the captain. "Apologize," you say. He shakes his head and you punch him in the mouth.

Immediately two of the other lieutenants leap up and grab your arms. You realize that you have struck a superior officer. You're going to be in a lot of trouble, even if they *don't* figure out you're a spy. You struggle to get away but they have you tight. The captain stands up and gets right in your face.

"That was a mistake, *madam*."

The captain and the others take you to another tent, where higher officers are meeting. Pickens tells them that he believes you are a woman — and a spy for the North. Your stomach sinks. If they convict you of being a spy, they will surely hang you.

Turn the page.

One of the many spies on both sides of the Civil War, Maria "Belle" Boyd began serving as a Confederate spy at age 17.

They quickly discover that you are a woman. But Pickens has no proof that you're a spy.

"We can't convict this girl as a spy without some proof," says one of the officers. Turning to you, he says, "You'd better get out of here. Go home and help the cause by making clothing or some other thing. There is plenty a woman can do to help our cause."

You change out of your uniform and leave the camp with nothing. You have no money, no food, no blankets, and no tent. You walk along the river for several days until you are discovered by Union scouts. When you tell them your story, they bring you to Washington, D.C. There, you learn that the Union Army is hiring women to be nurses. You sign up.

THE END

To follow another path, turn to page 9.
To read the conclusion, turn to page 101.

The doctor is right. In times of war, you have to make hard choices. Those who have a chance to live need your help more than those who are sure to die. You feel bad doing it but you leave the wailing man and join the doctor and the other patients.

You didn't notice it before, but the patients the doctor is attending to are both black men. One of them has fallen and has a broken leg. The other has a bayonet gash in his side. You bind the broken leg while the doctor dresses the other man's deep cut.

"Where have you come from?" you ask the man with the broken leg.

He shakes his head, afraid to speak.

"It's okay," you say. "I can help you."

Turn the page.

The man shuts his eyes in pain as you tighten the splint on his leg. When he opens them again, he says, "Beauregard's company. Our master sold us to the Rebel Army. We escaped when the fighting started."

"Stay here and rest," you say.

For the rest of the afternoon, you treat many dozens of injured men. Many of them die. Others walk out under their own power after having minor injuries treated. The doctor amputates arms and legs and outside the tent there is a large barrel loaded up with limbs. It is the most terrible day of your life.

That evening, when many of the patients are asleep, you see the black man with the broken leg standing. He is trying to lift his friend from the cot.

"You won't get far on that leg," you say. "And your friend can't go anywhere. He will start bleeding again if he moves around too much."

"We have to get out of here," the man says. "We won't go back to slavery."

You assure him that you will not let anyone arrest them here. He agrees to stay but only for one more day. The morning when they are ready to go, you give them what money you can. You also give them a couple of blankets and tell them the safest way to get to Washington, D.C. Watching them go, you feel a little better — as if this gruesome war might be worth it after all if you've helped save two men.

THE END

To follow another path, turn to page 9.
To read the conclusion, turn to page 101.

You can't bring yourself to leave the dying man, so you comfort him as best you can. You give him water and another dose of ether to ease his pain. Within 10 minutes, he dies peacefully. You're glad he did not die in agony but the doctor is furious with you. You are wasting valuable pain medication on a man who will not live. You are wasting time too. There are too many injured soldiers to treat to waste time with kindness.

You work hard the rest of the day but you feel the doctor's anger with you. After the battle is over, he fires you from your position. You are reassigned to the infantry where you become a soldier.

You think about the injured soldiers you saw in the hospital tent. So many were hurt, dying, or dead. Those who were unhurt were terrified of going back out to fight. To be a fighter is what you wanted in the first place, so maybe you should be glad. But now that you've seen the horrific reality of this war, you are filled with dread.

You could reveal yourself to be a woman — that would get you out of the fighting. But you also feel a sense of duty. You want more than ever to fight to preserve the Union and put an end to slavery. So you gather your gear and prepare for the next battle.

THE END

To follow another path, turn to page 9.
To read the conclusion, turn to page 101.

CHAPTER 5

A SIGN OF THE WAR TO COME

In July 1861, many Americans still believed that the Civil War might be not be very long or deadly. The North had advantages in number of troops and money as well as factories, food, horses, and railroads. For many, it seemed like these advantages would prove too much for the South to stand up against.

But the South was fighting a defensive battle. All they had to do was defend their territories and keep the North from a sustained invasion. Eventually, they believed, the Northerners would tire of fighting these difficult battles and give up.

The Confederate states were set to hold their Confederate Congress meeting on July 20 in Richmond, Virginia. President Abraham Lincoln wanted to take that city before this important meeting of the new Southern government could take place. So he had Brigadier General Irvin McDowell bring his army of 35,000 troops from Washington, D.C., to Manassas Junction at the Bull Run River. The plan, after winning there, was to continue to Richmond.

But McDowell's army made its way too slowly to Manassas Junction. In the meantime Confederate General Beauregard had been warned of the attack by a female spy. He was able to gather a large army there. He also called for backup troops from General Joseph E. Johnston.

Brigadier General Irvin McDowell

As the battle began, citizens, reporters, and politicians came out to picnic and watch what they believed would be an easy Union victory. It appeared that way at first. McDowell's army shelled the Confederates across the river and moved across it. They pushed the rebels up Henry House Hill. But by the afternoon, Johnston's reinforcements arrived. The Confederates forced the Union to retreat all the way back to Washington, D.C.

Hospital conditions during the war, and especially at the beginning of the war, were terrible. Doctors often operated without sterilizing — or even cleaning — their instruments. Wounded men often lay in the battlefields for days on end while their injuries became infected. Amputations were common.

Hospitals did not have enough instruments and tools. For example, at the start of the war there were only 20 thermometers on the entire Union side. After 1862 many women were hired as nurses, and conditions began to improve.

The Union lost about 3,000 men in the Battle of Bull Run, which was known as the Battle of Manassas in the South. The Confederates lost about 1,750. It was the first major battle of the Civil War and it was a decisive victory for the South. More than anything, it was a signal to everyone that this war would last a long time and many soldiers would die before it was over.

TIMELINE

June 29, 1861—President Abraham Lincoln meets with advisors to discuss war strategy; Brigadier General Irvin McDowell urges an attack on Confederate forces at Manassas Junction

July 16—McDowell's army leaves Washington, D.C.

July 17—Confederate General P. G. T. Beauregard, alerted to McDowell's advance, sends a message to General Joseph E. Johnston asking him to join him at Manassas to fight off the Union

July 18—Johnston begins loading troops onto the Manassas Gap Railroad to Manassas

July 19—Skirmishes begin between troops of Beauregard and McDowell

July 20—Johnston's troops have all arrived in Manassas

July 21, morning—Union soldiers attack, take control of Mathews Hill; Confederates retreat to Henry House Hill

July 21, afternoon—Confederates force Union soldiers into retreat; many panicked Union soldiers abandon the army and flee for home

July 22—Retreating Union armies reach Washington, D.C.

OTHER PATHS TO EXPLORE

In this book, you've seen how events from the past look different from three points of view. Perspectives on history are as varied as the people who lived it. Seeing history from many points of view is an important part of understanding it. Here are ideas for other Civil War points of view to explore:

* In 1862 President Abraham Lincoln's Preliminary Emancipation Proclamation opened the door for African-Americans to join the Union Army. What are some of the unique experiences and challenges black Union soldiers faced during the Civil War?

* The Civil War forced sweeping changes in the lives of American women. Some disguised themselves and fought while others served as nurses or spies. Many took on new duties at home when their male relatives became soldiers. Thousands of African-American women gained freedom. Using other texts or valid Internet sources, research the stories of at least two women whose lives were changed by the war.

READ MORE

Burgan, Michael. *Spies of the Civil War: An Interactive Espionage Adventure*. North Mankato, Minn.: Capstone Press, 2015.

Nardo, Don. *Civil War Witness: Mathew Brady's Photos Reveal the Horrors of War*. North Mankato, Minn.: Compass Point Books, 2014.

Thompson, Ben. *Guts & Glory: The American Civil War*. New York: Little, Brown and Company, 2014.

INTERNET SITES

Use FactHound to find Internet sites related to this book.

Visit *www.facthound.com*

Just type in 9781543502916 and go.

GLOSSARY

amputation (am-pyuh-TAY-shun)—the removal of an arm, leg, or other body part, usually because the part is damaged

artillery (ar-TIL-uh-ree)—cannons and other large guns used during battles

bayonet (BAY-uh-net)—a long metal blade attached to the end of a musket or rifle and used in hand-to-hand combat

Confederate (kuhn-FE-der-uht)—a person who supported the South during the Civil War

ether (EE-thuhr)—a liquid drug that used to be commonly used to make patients unconscious to deal with pain

infantry (IN-fuhn-tree)—a group of people in the military trained to fight on land

plantation (plan-TAY-shuhn)—a large farm where crops such as cotton and sugarcane are grown; before 1865, plantations were run by slave labor

rebel (REB-uhl)—someone who fights against a government or the people in charge of something; a nickname for Confederate soldiers during the Civil War

Yankee (YANG-kee)—a nickname for Union soldiers during the Civil War

BIBLIOGRAPHY

Davis, William C. *Battle at Bull Run: A History of the First Major Campaign of the Civil War*. Mechanicsburg, Penn.: Stackpole Books, 1995.

Franklin, John Hope, and Loren Schweninger. *Runaway Slaves: Rebels on the Plantation*. New York: Oxford University Press, 1999.

Keegan, John. *The American Civil War: A Military History*. New York: Vintage Books, 2010.

Robertson, James I. *Stonewall Jackson: The Man, the Soldier, the Legend*. New York: Macmillan Pub. USA, 1997.

Schultz, Jane E. *Women at the Front: Hospital Workers in Civil War America*. Chapel Hill, N.C.: University of North Carolina Press, 2004.

Symonds, Craig L. *Joseph E. Johnston: A Civil War Biography*. New York: Norton, 1992.

INDEX